God Refined

A Proposal for Peace

Robert A. Kezer

Copyright © 2006 by Robert A. Kezer
All rights reserved. No portion of this book may be reproduced – mechanically, electronically, or by any other means, including photocopying - without written permission of the author.

ISBN: 978-0-6151-3810-7

http://stores.lulu.com/bobkezer

godrefined@yahoo.com

First Edition, Revised.

Acknowledgements:

My gratitude to those who have offered critique on this project, and who have helped it come into being, especially: Zak, Jude, Skoj and Ellen; Lee, Dion, and my professors at the University of Oregon; and Professor Salim Yaqub, whose course, "The United States and the Middle East: 1914 to 9/11," was used for the historical time line in Part 4: Application of Principles: The Arab-Israeli Conflict. Thank you all.

*Mom,
Through this journey nothing has torn my heart more than
the pain I have caused you. I am sorry. Please forgive me.*

*I love you,
bobby*

Truth

–

Beauty

–

Goodness

Contents

	Page
Part 1: At Issue	1
Part 2: A Different Story	21
Part 3: Our Tools for Change	45
Part 4: Application of Principles: The Arab-Israeli Conflict	61

Part 1
At Issue

How do we create a better world – a place without warfare, genocide, and environmental destruction? Some of us charge this responsibility to our leaders while others expect their god to save those of their faith. Many more people feel they have no voice because they are only one among so many. These attitudes have held us back: today's problems are the result.

True change can only happen if we focus on elevating the fundamental basis from which we make our decisions. To not address our world's problems at the individual level means we continue to place the responsibility elsewhere: we are the face in the mirror, and recognizing this is our first step.

The premise in this book – and this has been offered by others – is that every decision we make is either based in love or results from fear. These two fundamental ways of relating to our world are the polar opposites that condition every action we take. On the surface they often seem similar, but at a deeper level they are much different.

One person embraces peace out of profound love for their neighbors: they have no desire for personal gain. Another acts in almost the same way but does so out of fear of retribution – either from some god, karmic debt, or belief in universal justice. While neither person hurts others, their motivation for not doing so is different. So are their levels of commitment to these principles guiding their conduct: fear does not serve us in our darkest hours. Only love can draw forth the passion needed to sustain our commitment to peace.

Fear based personalities stem from ancient concepts of God: this continues to direct much in our societies. Most people have been taught to fear their creator – to believe in hell, damnation, and God's wrath. For them it is logical to believe that if there is a god, then this god will judge, condemn, and punish us upon death for our infractions during life: there is good and evil and whether we understand this or not, we are held responsible. They then copy this pattern into their lives, our society, and the global institutions dictating our existence.

Today we have a world economic system that continues to allow 800 million souls a year remain chronically malnourished – not because we do not have the food to feed them, but because they do not have the money to buy it. Placing the quest for power above all else has resulted in profit becoming more important than people: we have allowed, and continue to see happen, the wholesale eradication of most of the indigenous cultures that once thrived in our world.

Tradition has been overwhelmed by progress leaving a legacy of genocide in its wake. With little thought given to our collective responsibility as stewards of the planet, many people have selfishly taken all they could and left almost nothing for future generations – their inheritance is a destroyed environment they cannot repair, only adapt to. Rather than accepting our individual responsibility for this, we often claim impotence and blame others.

We are disconnected from the institutions framing our world: what is correct personal conduct gives way to power based policy. The whole does not represent the parts: truth, fairness, and responsibility - necessary attributes for a healthy family - are not the guiding principles of our world community. Perpetuating the economic model, not recognizing our interdependence, dominates our reasoning. We have the obligation to expect better.

At the family level we promote the improved welfare of our offspring, while in the global sphere we allow our leaders to legislate in ways that destroy their future. People of high moral character are promoted as models to exemplify, yet these traits are not appropriate foreign policy. We are expected to obey the rule of law for the greater benefit of all, while our leaders maintain a global system of anarchy where the biggest stick rules.

Some people argue that without fear humanity would never have advanced – that it was necessary for strong leaders to command loyalty. This may be true, or not: all we know for sure is that we have never tried another way. Fear has always reigned in our collective consciousness. This grants that at some level anger and impatience, criticism and judgment, and violence and revenge – the common fare of today's global stage – become acceptable.

Concepts of scarcity, superiority, and religious intolerance dominate our cultures. Competition overrides cooperation in almost every area. It seems that no matter how much we have desired a better world, we have always allowed that for one group to have, another must not. Do we really wish to continue like this?

Our other option is to release the fear that holds us back, generate the necessary momentum for change, and then create an environment conditioned by love. To make this happen enough people need to believe the very essence of God is love. When we know God as perfection of love we realize that anger –the worst of human emotions - can never be attributed to this deity.

God has never gotten mad or impatient or lashed out at creation: these beliefs come from the days when sacrifice was routine. We know better now. To believe that after death we are greeted by an empathetic, compassionate, and merciful divine parent – one that loves us, understands our natural failings, and who forgives us for them – releases us. We begin to live our lives with joy, abandon, and excitement absent the criticism, judgment, and inevitable violence of the past.

Embracing our unity – realizing we are all siblings of the same divine creator - removes the idea that some people are more worthy than others because of wealth, religion, or ethnicity. We are all children of the same family: we have an obligation to help each other.

We have experienced the truth that for any of us to suffer hurts us all. Just as we would ensure that all of the members of our personal family are cared for, we need to have consideration for those living in hardship around the world. Our disparities in wealth, resources, and education need to be reduced. If not, what can we expect to happen when those without similar opportunity demand their accounting?

When the people who have more begin to care for those who have less, we will heal. This accelerates when people gifted with greater abilities use more of their energy for humanity's welfare, rather than their own gain.

It is time to drop our grudges: we all bear a degree of responsibility. It may not be right to forget everything that has happened, but it is essential for us to forgive. Seldom a rapid process, this is not one we often wish to begin: many times we expect the other person to apologize first. We allow ourselves to be controlled by our emotions, which come from our human side, and not our feelings, which stem from the Divine.

We act out of fear when we try to insure our place in

life by accumulating material things: we hoard, become static, and hope to buy our way out of any problem. Holding on to our stuff becomes more important than anything else. We learn to only associate with those of similar status: people's bank accounts start to mean more than their characters. This process separates us from each other and our common heritage: we turn into fortified islands built to hold off the rest of humanity.

Love though, is a reciprocal process of giving and receiving that increases in quantity and quality with each cycle. We cannot receive love and keep it, only bask in its healing effect as it flows through us and on to others.

Love allows us to release our hold on the material. We live with greater spontaneity trusting more in the relationships we foster. Our true rewards do not come from riches, but from the return of loving consideration we first spread ourselves. This provides us our best security in an uncertain world, and forever conditions our memories of this first life. As we have been told, it is in the giving that we receive.

Can we ever achieve a more equitable distribution of the world's resources without fairness becoming a guiding principle? Should violence – whether physical, passive, or social – be tolerated any longer, or can we replace it with dialog, consensus, and understanding?

For the first time in history we have a framework of belief that allows us - with intent - to reach for a higher level of conduct. As some people break the generational cycles that have destroyed their families, we can change the historical trends that define us. In doing so we achieve a greater revelation of God and remake ourselves in that divine image.

With the god of this presentation, every meaningful action is scaled by the degree of eternal truth, divine beauty, and infinite goodness it contains. Little in our world is black or white. Evil is not a force in and of itself, but rather the degree to which these traits are missing. Knowing this helps us learn how to live, act toward others, and shape our future global government.

Only by gaining a more refined image of God can we both follow our hearts and trust our actions are grounded in love. Using these criteria to judge whether thoughts we consider from God are valid helps us to separate divine guidance from human garbage. Would a loving parent ever tell one of their children to harm the others in their family? To think God would, is absurd. This misunderstanding has brought much horror, and no longer is this teaching appropriate.

The power of choice is ours. As people increase the number of love-based decisions they make, they change. Those who have done this know the process cannot be rushed: each of us must have the time to fail, reassess, and experience the eventual outcome of our efforts. Wisdom is knowledge combined with experience, which is not gained just from greater time on planet, but through the active process of making difficult choices.

As with the parts, so goes the whole: as more people change, so does our world. Like with the balance beam scale held by the lady of justice, every decision counts. Each positive choice has weight and works to affect the momentum directing our planet. At first we are unable to see the progress: the other side has great weight and movement will not happen until we almost reach equilibrium. Then everything accelerates, good over takes bad, and peace comes to the Earth.

Bringing forth a new system is a process: we allow the old to fade as the new takes form. Our hope resides with better choices being made by a new generation, not converting those in charge now. People seldom change when they want to, much less when they do not. With time, room is made for those with a different vision.

Our children need a world in which the results of their choices are clear. Fear has left its legacy: we must now build ours. Anything we use to create our future will remain a part of it. This means not placing our focus on fighting what is wrong, but rather on promoting what is right - people putting their time, money, and energy into love-based action. To do otherwise is to remain anchored in the past using anger, animosity, and personal indignation against ourselves.

Who does not feel these fear-based emotions when they lash out in protest? How can pitting hate against hate ever work? Our energy stems from a different source: we do not want to try and use theirs against them. When we do, we seldom see progress.

A different outcome requires new tactics: not knowing this defines us as insane. Fear is the disease and the greater issues in our world are its symptoms: by channeling our energy in positive ways we cure it rather than manage it.

This book is about a new way to know our Creator: its purpose is not to convert. People are urged to use this information to augment their current forms of worship. We are speaking of an enhanced personal relationship with God, not the competition that wages between the churches.

Religious diversity is not our problem: antagonism, spiritual stagnation, and thoughts of superiority are. People of all religions can use this information to achieve a better understanding of God, their relationship with their Creator, and our responsibility to be good stewards of the planet – and the better we know this, the closer we all become.

Dogma anchors our religious institutions in the past: they have not evolved as we have. Modern minds are being forced into ancient constructs: doctrine has not kept pace with science. This disparity between our spiritual level and our technological ability has limits: we must reduce the tension before it destroys us.

Truth is not static: it changes as we grow in awareness. Our duty is to redefine it as we gain maturity, experience, and knowledge. Only in this way do we progress. As it becomes more refined we learn to apply it with greater dexterity.

Should we not expect the same from our world's faiths? Do they not have an obligation to incorporate the wisdom garnered over the ages into the teachings they promote? Somehow, we must both honor our founding documents, and still allow for change as we mature.

There is a way to believe in God that inspires hope, is inclusive of everyone, and allows for our daily increases in scientific knowledge. Yes, eternal life is freely offered to all and should be accepted as such. No, we do not go from being gross, material, and imperfect mortals one moment, to sitting with God the next. Ours is a long journey to the center, our deaths are nothing more than portals, and we are always expected to strive for increased awareness: never do we gain outside of our own efforts.

This is written with the hope of causing as little antagonism as possible to others of different beliefs – the source material stands on its own and does not require contrast with other religions for validity. Some statements are in direct contradiction with what other people profess: this cannot be helped. The god within is one of love, divine mercy, and absolute perfection: a loving parent, not stern judge. This is not an extension of the ancient god of wrath.

The degree of our own faith is shown by how much we allow others to practice theirs. Intolerance shows ignorance of the unified nature of our existence. God never requires us to harm others. People who embrace this creator do not justify violence under the guise of religion.

This presentation speaks of Jesus Christ and accepts his divine nature, but it is not based on the New Testament. It does not support primary Christian doctrine such as hell, original sin, or Christ dying for us.

The founders of Christianity were not perfect. Being Jews first, their faith bound them to the belief that a messiah was coming to sit on the throne of David, vanquish their enemies, and create an earthly kingdom where they ruled over the gentiles. The apostles were not able to understand Christ's message that the kingdom of God was spiritual, that it was within the heart of the believer, and that this salvation was offered to all people regardless of religion, ethnicity, or social status.

Because of these misunderstandings, compromises were made. The church founders worked to develop a religion about Christ - one based on the fact that he rose from the dead - rather than a religion of what he taught. These errors conditioned their subsequent writings, and hence, many people's understanding of God. Their books were later translated across time and into modern languages making them at best approximations of the original content. The result has been contradiction, animosity between sects, and doctrine unacceptable to many people: it has not brought our world peace.

This book relates to a different accounting of events – not all of it, just the essential parts necessary to help us better understand our Creator. It is based on a document known as the Urantia Revelation that is published as the book and by the foundation bearing that name. Compiled during the first half of the 20th Century, it was understood that the material would not gain acceptance immediately: it would take a later generation to understand its message.

The people involved with the origination of the material are shrouded in secrecy. The official claim is this stops any human from being revered by future generations. Other sources state the information is the response to questions asked by a group formed to investigate a person who, when asleep, would speak as other personalities.

The text generated claims celestial authorship from a wide array of spiritual entities commissioned to transmit the revelation. It says that our world has had unique problems, that we have gone off track, and that this special group is to help us correct the situation. Humanity is considered responsible, free choice of will is emphasized, and growth requires our active participation: we cannot know our divine nature by being told about it, we must experience the process.

Information new to us – revelation - was only given when nothing else already in our knowledge bank could be used. Because of this, the work contains over one thousand of humanity's highest concepts of religious and philosophical thought. Meeting the commission's mandate meant the material would not be perfect, but only offer that level of truth needed for us to regain our spiritual path. Also, human beings were involved in transcribing the work: as has always happened before, errors occurred in the process.

Controversy surrounds all books that support the various religions: the Urantia Revelation is no exception. Skeptics question many things, including how the revelation came to be, its claim of celestial authorship, and its lack of moral dictates. Upon review, though, of the stories offered by others, like virgin births, the infallibility of human writings, and the inevitable floods sent by angry gods, this one seems to be at least as reasonable.

Unsettling to some is the way the Urantia Revelation strips power from those who today claim religious authority. It supports a secular world government, rejects notions of chosen people, and calls for women – at every level - to become full partners in the world's decision-making process. It states that only when one religion claims to be superior to another that religious wars – or those promoted by religious people - can break out. History teaches that all institutions have survival instincts that make them fight to maintain their authority at almost any cost. No matter how this material is presented, there will be those who feel threatened by it.

No priest, church, or institution can ever come between a person and God. It states that religion is personal and defines our individual relationship with our Creator. Concepts of excommunication, ecclesiastical authority, or another person's spiritual inferiority are invalid. Women have absolute equality with men.

People are urged to pray to God, but they are also advised to do so when alone, in their own words, and for spiritual growth not material gain. Developing a child/parent relationship with God is important. Churches are said to be social groups for people who wish to be with others of similar beliefs. This fellowship is encouraged, but belonging to a specific church confers no increased worth upon the person.

The Urantia Revelation fills a massive volume containing 2097 pages of 8 ½ by 11- inch biblical paper with over one million words. It is unreasonable to expect people who just want to know its essential message to read the entire book. Yet, never before has the world needed its help as it does now.

Have we ever been more at risk - whether from nuclear weapons, unrestrained consumption, or the harm we have done to our world's environment – than we are now? Has there ever been a time when it was more important to understand our relationships with others, and is that knowledge not linked to how we view our Creator? The world may not have been ready to accept direct spiritual intervention on our behalf fifty years ago, but it seems to be yearning for it today.

This revelation offers a path to abolishing warfare. Nothing is more important if we want to solve the global problems threatening our existence. If correct – and that is best shown through the words, lives, and actions of those believing it - then it needs to be broken down for greater access by more people.

Everyone has their own method of learning that works best for them, whether by reading, listening to recordings, or gathering to hear someone speak. It is the duty of those spreading this message to accommodate that diversity. If a person has further interest, they can then tackle the original document.

Never should we allow the lesser to take precedence over the greater: more important than someone reading a complex cosmology is the simple knowledge that God is within us, we are within God, creation is bound by divine love, and mercy is offered to all who want it. This is the message that moves us into the era of peace.

Freedom of religious thought – the choice of how to believe or even the decision not to believe – always stays with the person. If there is a creator, and that being does not force us to believe in it, then no earthly power has the right to either. There have always been many diverse religions: throughout history people have found love, peace, and the path to eternal life in most of them, as have atheists and those who claim no religious preference at all. Not respecting this right of choice is the way of the spiritual imposters - those who promote their will, not God's, through hate, anger, and violence.

To create a space for our children where religious diversity is embraced and all faiths are equal under a sovereign Creator, we need to draft the documents stating this. Our planet is ready for a religious treaty: an agreement that is signed, adhered to, and promoted by new groups in each faith. Doctrine and practice we know to be harmful need to be modified: letting the past control our future ensures our destruction. Each religion will remain unique, but no longer can we embrace wording or ceremony that teaches hate, places one group over another, or condones violence as a means to an end.

This is a requisite step: peace will not come from a miracle but rather our own efforts. We must make the leap of faith: like a free climber on a shear cliff with no choice but up, we need to have the courage to jump for our next handhold. To not act means we fall and suffer the consequences. Breaking free from the institutions of the past may seem like an extreme measure, but they no longer meet our needs. If we continue in the same way, how can we ever expect different results?

Part 2

A Different Story

Humans are part of the material realm of time and space. The worlds of these universes are where potential souls are born, personalities developed, and survival instincts firmed. As biological beings we have evolved, as have all other species. Evolution, whether according to Darwin's theory or another, is happening.

Sometime during our first several years most of us developed the ability to choose between right and wrong: this differs us from an animal mind. It means we have become creatures capable of choosing God's will: we can form eternal souls. At the instant we made our first moral choice, a part of God entered our minds and a process of spiritualization began.

We are finite: we have a beginning and an end. By ourselves we cannot comprehend concepts of eternity, infinity, and universality. To know God, we must experience love, and our divine guide leads us through the process. This portion of our ultimate Creator, that entity from the First Great Source and Center, speaks to us as that quiet voice in our heart.

After a period of time, whether this happens during the mortal life or in one of those to come, the developing personality can reach the full, free, and unreserved choice to do God's will. This is when the two sides, the human and the Divine, meld. This fusion forms a new eternal being, a soul, and never again will the two separate.

Sometime after death we are brought to a point of decision: do we wish to continue on with eternal life doing God's will, or not? This choice is freely given and should be received as such. No one has any price to pay for being here, no one is born in sin, and everyone is invited to continue the journey.

Once eternal life has been accepted, spiritual progression happens through individual self-effort. It is not reasonable to think we can have human failings one moment, and lose them the next just because we die. We are expected to seek our divine legacy.

God does not send us to hell for punishment, nor purgatory to become redeemed, nor heaven to live a life of ease. This does not mean that the willful transgression of God's laws do not have consequences: they do. But rather than God judging and then condemning us, the seeds of our own destruction are inherent within our choices. Each one either moves us closer to, or farther away, from God.

Every time we choose against divine will, we harden ourselves and increase the chance we will do so again: the pattern becomes set over time. We become cynical, sarcastic, and intolerant – our emotions dominate our feelings and we lose our ability to love our neighbor. When these people are given the choice to go on, they decide not to.

When a personality rejects our Creator's gift of eternal life, annihilation occurs. The entity of God within the person takes all of value that ever happened in that life, and then returns to its source: nothing good is ever wasted. The human personality then becomes as if it never was, just like any other animal mind that dies.

No matter how far removed from God a potential soul becomes, any flicker of desire for forgiveness will be answered. Each of us has more mercy available than we could ever require: none who desire eternal life will ever be turned away.

Wherever a person leaves off down here, at that exact level they start again. Some of us may have longer, more rigorous journeys to endure, but all can participate. In this way everything is in alignment: free will reigns; eternal life is freely given; justice, fairness, and mercy correlate; spiritual evolution stems from personal decisions, and never is there cause for us to fear our divine parent.

Those who accept God's gift enter into a progressive system of training and bodily transformation. We do not go from the material directly to the spiritual: we must grow into it. While the spiritual can access the material, the material cannot know the spiritual. This next period helps us resolve our failings, teaches us our place in the celestial hierarchy, and readies us to go forth in joy doing our Creator's will.

The intervening space between the material and the spiritual is known as the morontia. This is the home of the mansion worlds, hundreds of progressive training spheres created for us to journey through during successive incarnations. Ours is a process of transformation: each new body is made of finer matter as we lose the vestiges of our human failings and take on divine traits.

Incarnating from here to somewhere else is the only way we do not limit God to human reasoning. There is no bank of souls that can ever be emptied. None of us – at least our personalities - has existed before, and we do not keep coming back to this sphere for endless cycles of life. These are concepts created by finite minds: humans attempting to make sense the premonitions they feel, but don't understand.

Only by allowing for unlimited biological procreation can mortal limits of our Creator be removed. If we all kept coming back to the same planet over and over, there could only be so many of us. This keeps the numbers within our conceptual ability, but it suggests God is static rather than an evolutionary being. Spiritual progression through a series of lives occurs, just not back to this world.

Accounts of people having the sense they have lived before have occurred throughout time. This may be other than it seems. Those potential souls that have rejected eternal life freed the entity of God within them. This being was then able to later pair with another mind in its quest to form a new soul. In this process images from other lives lived by this spirit may transfer to the new person they invest. What we sense is not that we have lived before, but rather that the God within us may of had other life experiences before ours.

We are bound to each other through these entities stemming from the eternal: God knows all and they are God. Everything that has happened, is now occurring, or will take place on the material world, is concurrent in the spiritual. While our abilities differ, all of us at some level can access our eternal side. Knowing about our unified nature helps us understand that some people may glimpse images from elsewhere they think to be their own.

From our ultimate Creator came all matter, but this divine parent did not create the material worlds. This belief causes the major problem inherent in all religions: if God is benevolent and all-powerful, then why are so many people suffering? If our Creator is perfect, should not all manifested by God also be perfect? This contradiction between God being perfect and our world suffering can only be explained by placing us outside of God's direct control: our Creator delegates as we do.

God is perfect, but the material realm is not: there is universal justice, but accidents happen. In confusion, we base our understanding of God's love on earthly events: we pattern the infinite after the finite. Just because people harm each other does not mean God harms us. Rather, a perfect being allowed imperfect souls to be created so they, through their own free choice of will, could achieve perfection and join with that Creator.

Those in the material can never prove the existence of the spiritual: the finite cannot measure the eternal. Nor is that our purpose. As our science advances we learn more about our planet, our universe, and ourselves - essential knowledge for solving today's problems.

Science and belief in an ultimate creative force – God – do not have to contradict: people can embrace their spiritual urgings without having to discount their education. The research showing the age of our world, the evolution of species, and the fact there is no genetic basis to the concept of race, is solid.

The big bang theory suggests all matter is exploding forth from what was at one time a tiny speck of condensed energy. At the molecular level we are taught there is vast space between the actual particles that make up the material world. It seems our science is telling us that what was once dense, has become diffused. But from where did that original explosion - containing within itself the stuff of billions of worlds - come?

Imagine God residing at the center of a spiritual dimension of absolute perfection that dwarfs all of material creation. From a creative outburst a pinprick opened in the fabric of God's domain: in an instant our universe burst forth into unorganized space. This material is still shooting outward to fill what we know as the material realm.

When we observe creation we do so seeing only one side of the event. It seems reasonable that this manifestation of divine energy would look like what our scientists explain as big bang.

We come from God and God is within us, but we exist outside of the realm where our Creator resides. The stuff of which we are made comes from the First Source, but we are not source-like: the atoms of creation came from perfection, but the universe is not perfect. The material and the spiritual are separate - two distinct domains.

Stuff from the material cannot reside in the spiritual. The spiritual though, can enter the material: the presence of God within us is perfect, does come from the original source, and will guide us to our Creator as we become more like the divine.

A Different Story

As we grow in perfection, God grows. Evolution continues, for those perfect as well as those not: to stop growing is to die. Our existence is not only for us, but to also serve as an experiential event for God. When this space known as the material realm becomes perfected, as is the spiritual, it becomes one with it: all is assimilated and God increases in scope.

On millions upon millions of worlds there are trillions upon trillions of mortals being born, each one a potential new soul. Our relationship with God allows each of us to be both portals through which our Creator's love can flow into our universe, and focal points for God to experience creation. In this way the loop is complete: the greatest is intimately tied to the least and no others can intervene.

The task of organizing this matter into the universes of time and space was delegated to the creator siblings. Of God and one with God, each is distinct from God. They come forth from the spiritual realm, muster the material of space, and create the celestial hierarchy to administer their universes.

These divine children are, for all intents and purposes, the Gods of their particular space. Worship – loving communion with our Creator when no request is involved –

should be reserved for God. It is from God that we all have the opportunity for eternal life. Prayer, a spiritual request of some sort, should be sent to the sovereign of the universe: for us, that is Jesus Christ.

In the process of bringing a universe to completion, these creator children are required to incarnate several times into various orders of beings within their celestial hierarchy. This is required to gain full sovereignty over their domains: they are expected to know their universe, as do those inhabiting it. One reason Christ came to our world was to complete this series of incarnations, this time as a mortal.

How Christ could incarnate as a babe on a world of time and space is a mystery to even those above. Not everything of God is known. But what we do know is that nothing unusual occurred with the birth of Christ: Mary conceived in the normal fashion.

Virgin birth stories were common in the ancient world. They promote the idea that women are impure - that either having sex with them, or passing through their vaginal canal, is something that degrades the spiritual worth of a man or god.

Gender is a part of this plane, but no other. Neither

God nor any in the celestial hierarchy should be referred to as male or female. Christ incarnated as a man because of the era in which he came, not because men are in any way superior to women. He had to bring his message forth from within the existing social structure, and this would have been much more difficult for him to do as a woman.

God makes no distinction based on gender. To allow ideas of male superiority to remain in our scriptures means to perpetuate them - that at some level we accept them as valid. Men have kept these institutions in place, but women also have responsibility. What would bring about change more quickly than our sisters just refusing to participate in groups that do not recognize their absolute equality?

The person we know as Jesus Christ was both a son of humanity and a Son of God. For us to interact with this level of being he needed to reduce himself to our level – to become material. Christ said that those who have seen him have witnessed our Creator, but he did not say that he was God.

The idea that Christ was sent here to die for humanity's sins extends the ancient Jewish sacrificial system. Once again, humans built God in their image. The idea that our Creator would send its beloved child to be killed for our sake is abhorrent to many people, and nothing has hindered the spreading of the gospel of Christ more than this idea. Crucifying Christ did not meet the divine criteria of eternal truth, divine beauty, and infinite goodness.

It was God's will that Christ live out his life in the flesh to demonstrate the love of our Creator and the siblinghood of humanity: he was to do this without using his divine powers if at all possible. It was his to exemplify adherence to God's will: we are to have faith, not to expect the outward show of miracles. The inability of the people living then to understand the message he brought reflects their failings, not his, God's, or humanity's.

We are expected to grow into our spiritual status: we can be taught, but not forced to learn. Christ had nothing to fear from us, and did not. He carried out God's will allowing others to make their own choices. While people killed Christ, to think that we, the finite, could ever hurt Christ, the eternal, is the height of arrogance.

Christ brought us the assurance of the parenthood of God and the subsequent siblinghood of humanity. He taught that the kingdom of God was within each of us. He lived a life of peace, tolerance, and patience. While at one time he told the apostles to love others as they loved themselves – the sixth level of the famous Golden Rule - he later stated that this was not even enough: they were commanded to love others as God would have them love the person.

Regardless of how we wish to be treated, or how the other is acting, we are supposed to base our relationships in love. If someone wishes to harm us or those we have the ability to help, we use that force necessary to stop them and nothing more.

Judgment and any punishment must only come from those officials our society as a whole has delegated to that task. As individuals, we are to treat others with tolerance, patience, compassion, and good will: no longer can anger, revenge, or retribution be considered appropriate.

Christ is known to have said that the way to our Creator is through him. He was present on the planet and speaking in person to those considering his message. What we think is plain may not be. For people of later generations, especially those educated in the intrigue, contradictions, and horrible acts attributed to almost all religions, it does not seem fair that we have to choose the right faith to reach God.

If this were the case, then only those who choose Christianity would receive eternal life, yet even within this faith there is dissention about who will be saved. To believe one way is the only way is to believe everyone else is wrong. This means we think God sees other people as less than us, a tactic that has been used to justify almost every war.

Christ wanted us to first worship God, and this happens in many different ways. Yes, it is presented that he was the one delegated to create us, and if true, then it is obvious that a soul goes through Christ to reach our mutual parent. This does not mean, though, that a human being must understand all of this now: given the confusion on this planet that would be absurd. Our universe is fair: different cultures require their own ways of belief.

When we come to the point of decision after death we are more cognizant of our surroundings. We have knowledge of our afterlife, not just belief in it. Nothing is more important than our worship of God, including our acceptance during mortal life of the divine nature of Christ. To say otherwise is to place the lesser before the greater.

Believing in God must come first: this keeps a person's soul safe. When God is understood as perfect truth, beauty, and goodness, it keeps our world safe. This is happening in almost all religions. Fine-tuning our understanding of everything else can, and does, happen later.

This is the only way we can promote the equality of all faiths under a single sovereign Creator - the understanding that no religion is superior to any other. None of us has perfect knowledge of God: all of our teachings, including this one, have errors, but most of these ways also contain some truth. Our hope requires us to embrace those higher concepts that bring us closer, and to sever those ideas fueling antagonisms from the past.

Three days after being crucified, Christ ascended. He then reappeared in a series of visitations to various groups of people. He did not show himself in a resurrected material body. That was disposed of by the angels tasked to that duty, for no other reason than they did not want to witness the decomposition of their Creator's body: his death was enough.

During his one life in the flesh Christ achieved that oneness of soul where the material melds with the spiritual – he showed us the perfection of life in this sphere. When he reappeared to speak with his followers, it was in the bodies of the morontia realm. Each time they saw him, he was a little different: finer in composition, more spiritual than material, and more difficult for the people to discern. During this period Christ traversed all of the same levels of attainment that we will: in all ways this creator child was tried as we are.

Christ did say that he would return to our planet some day: he did not say when this would be. Never did Christ connect his return to ideas about the end of the world. Yet, both Islam and Christianity claim that this Prince of Peace – divine love manifested into human form with never a mean word attributed to him – will return to lead them to victory in the final battle against the other. This leaves our world in a dangerous position.

There is no fight between good and evil: these are manifestations of our imperfect selves. There is that of God, and that not: the more of one, the less of the other. There is an inverse relationship between the amount of evil that can be present and the level of divinity in any situation.

We cannot fight against evil because evil is defined as an absence of God. To do so decreases even further God's presence - resistance uses traits not of the divine, but of us. This is like throwing gasoline on a fire and with similar results: we become consumed by the inferno of emotions driving our conduct. When the tools of fear such as anger, violence, and greed are used to achieve something, they remain the essence of it.

To reduce evil in our world we need to increase the presence of what we know to be of God – eternal truth, divine beauty, and infinite goodness. Using love – demonstrated as patience, compassion, and fairness - we will negotiate our way to a better world one decision at a time. We remain focused in the present, not allowing our past to destroy us, nor our future to overwhelm us. What was idealism before now becomes reality.

No outside force opposes God. When a universe is brought to perfection, God's presence is unified throughout the entire creation. Anything less than this means the universe is imperfect – that it has pockets of space where God's presence is less than total. These gaps in the whole – areas where the perfection of God is lacking – are what we call evil.

Absolute evil is a complete lack of God's presence: everything else is relative. Absence of God is a void, one that can only be filled with love: anything else present signifies a lack of it. To know this is to understand the key to forgiveness.

Not all minds develop the ability to discern right from wrong: this is different than intelligence. These minds never become invested with God's presence because they have never shown the capacity to do divine will. Upon death these energy patterns dissipate, as would an animal's, but while functioning on Earth they may have been responsible for some of humanity's most heinous episodes.

Those entities known as the devil, Lucifer, Satan, and Beelzebub all existed: whether or not they still do is open for debate. These were created beings within the celestial hierarchy administering our universe who went into rebellion. Everywhere free choice of will reigns supreme: the ability to choose God's way means we also have the capacity to do otherwise.

The rebellion led by Lucifer included the spiritual being overseeing the evolution of our planet. This entity is the one that became known as the devil. This fallen child of light cannot influence us unless we wish it to. None of those who were part of the rebellion are now causing us our problems.

Even with the possibility of one of our celestial leaders going astray, we have the assurance of divine guidance through the portion of God within us. The beings administering our universe are created entities that are born knowing God exists: they believe because they know. Being imperfect themselves, some have rebelled and misguided those under their charge.

Does it seem fair that we who must proceed on faith

would not be given a means to determine what is not correct? Mortals are born on the material worlds without proof of God's existence. Instead, God is in us, and through the exhibition of faith, we advance that relationship. While others, whether human or not, may use better reasoning to sway our thoughts, we can use the intuitive impulse of our Creator within to steer us clear of danger.

The celestial overseers of many other planets were also part of the rebellion. This disunity – a challenge to God's will – reduced the presence of Deity within the greater universe: always, the degree of God present is based upon the level of acceptance of divine will. Because of the negative effect this group of planets had on the rest of our creation, the worlds involved were placed into spiritual quarantine. Our actions could not be allowed to harm the rest of the universe.

This spiritual isolation drew our world into the state of confusion we know as our collective history. Throughout this time periodic revelations have been made to help us maintain the concept of monotheism – the understanding that there is only one ultimate creator deity rather than many gods competing for our loyalty. The Urantia revelation was the last of these attempts.

We were told that we were entering into an era of

materialism that would threaten our existence: we can see this now. Christ said that his gospel would lead the world to peace, but also that it would be a long time in coming. Our helpers say our world will find the spiritual era, but not when. Accomplishing this is our responsibility: how are we going to redirect the momentum driving us to destruction?

Foremost is for more people to understand that God is a loving creator parent, one under which all religions are equal. Our transformation from fear to love is a process, not an event: as we refine how we believe in God, we change how we act. Love is not taught, but experienced: it is self-perpetuating - the more put forth in the world, the more we receive back. This provides us the sustenance for change.

Ideas of nationalism must cease: no longer can nation states possess the unbridled right to wage war. The only fair way to exist peacefully is through a global representative democracy constrained by a universal declaration of human rights. Everyone in the world has the same right to the life, liberty, and the pursuit of happiness that has been championed by the United States.

As people have learned to give greater loyalty to their nation than their local community, so must we now grow into world citizenship. We can all remain unique cultures, but at some level we must also recognize the greater global family of which we are a part. Hopes of regaining past glories must end: it is time for us to unify in the present. Issues such as poverty, starvation, and over population are localized events resulting from unequal representation on the global stage.

Understood today is the devastating influence of corporate greed. Business has bought all political leaders: to remain elected they must bow to their donor's will. Non-state actors – economic organizations outside of the voting process - dictate policy to our world's governments: a few benefits at the expense of the many. We have always known our answers can be found at the end of the money trail, but do we have the courage now to challenge what we find?

Pure capitalism is a beast of ever increasing efficiency: it must continue to grow to survive. It is an economic system, not a way of being: its goal is profit, not an enhanced life. Its laws are finite, not eternal. When uncaged, it runs like an engine without a governor, going faster and faster until it melts down.

Our world only has so many resources – at some point this monster will run out of fuel and begin to consume itself. We do not have the right, though, to steal our world from future generations. Profit is not progress, per se, and neither one should be placed before people or the planet. Doing so puts the desires of a few over the needs of the rest. Competition has its place, but only within certain bounds.

Pure democracy does not work: it means 51% of the people can dictate life to the other 49%. The only fair way is to constrain democracy with a bill of rights that protects individual freedoms from the collective will. Capitalism also requires similar controls. Competition and free market theory need parameters that limit a corporation's quest for profit: left to themselves they have destroyed much of our planet.

The collective welfare of humanity and the effect on the local community where business happens must come first. This requires that corporate rights be reduced to less than those of any of the world's citizens: the least of us is more important than any company's desire for profit.

To achieve global peace – that point where war is abolished as a means to an end - requires that women share equally in the decision making process, from raising the family to managing our planet. So far, men have made most decisions of import: the chaos on the world is our doing. It is time we accept this responsibility and offer our sisters equal representation at the table.

Christ made no differentiation between the spiritual worth of men and women: all are considered equal under God's eyes. Jesus was specific in this teaching, and he had many women involved in his ministry. After the crucifixion church founders reverted to their old ways and took back from women their newly found freedom. Change comes slowly, especially when it means one group has to relinquish power held over another.

Men and women are two sides of the same race. For peace, both must participate equally. This requires that greater consideration – opportunity - be offered to those marginalized now until the transition to balance is achieved.

These approaches are more easily discussed than accomplished. They require us to release the institutions of the past – ways based in fear – and create a new existence, one of love. This means those controlling the world now – or others like them - will not do so in the future. They will though, fight to survive.

Love inspires, fear destroys: positive actions must replace negative reactions. Only love can generate the passionate intensity we need to survive this journey. Tolerance, forgiveness, and community need to be taught, then experienced, and finally adopted. Patience will be required.

The vision for the next generation must be lived: we need to demonstrate that of which we speak. Those seeking positive change should unify themselves: competition is the way of fear, cooperation the way of love. Never before has the world had the chance it does today. How though, do we apply these principles and use this window of opportunity to offer a new era of global leadership?

Part 3

Our Tools for Change

When God forgives us it is our Creator's acceptance of our faith in divine mercy: this allows us to enter the spiritual kingdom. Our mistakes vanish: they are not held over our head as an imposition of guilt. Divine forgiveness is inevitable. Never is penance or sacrifice demanded.

No one is perfect: we will all require forgiveness. As we better understand God, we repent our mistakes: we acknowledge going against divine will, offer apology for doing so, and commit to acting better next time. After confession we should feel no guilt: doing so shows a lack of faith in God's mercy.

Our capacity to receive God's forgiveness is created in our souls when we forgive others: the love God offers us, we must pass on. Our Creator forgives us even before we ask for it, but we only experience this in our personal relationship with God when we in turn forgive. This is not an option for those who chose eternal life, but a requirement. Cessation of existence does not happen because God refuses to forgive us, but because we refuse to accept our Creator's mercy on faith.

To forgive is divine, a manifestation of God's love: hate, anger, and revenge are human emotions, the demonstration of mortal fear. Our relationship with our Creator is similar to us with our children: what mother has ever needed to forgive a 3 year-old child for their mistakes? Having to do so would be ridiculous. How could they not know that their child's errors are nothing more than part of the learning process, even if the child does not understand, confess, or repent? With God it is the same.

To forgive is to transcend our emotions: it requires an understanding of our unity, our divine nature, and our personal relationship with God. Forgiving moves us closer to God: holding our grudges reverses the process. Love advances our spiritual self-worth: hate destroys us. The more love in the world, the better for everyone: the more fear, the worse off everyone's plight. Again, it is in the giving that we receive.

We achieve our highest state when we love everyone as our Creator would have us do: from this stems our best conduct. The more intimate our understanding of others, the easier it is for us to love them, which is to have already forgiven: in this way we model God. To not forgive others shows the degree of a person's spiritual immaturity - their inability to be God-like.

Our journey is to perfection: along the way, all vestiges of our mortal selves must be replaced with the attributes of divinity. This transformation requires intention – a commitment to remaining grounded in love-based action. Change is often slow: knowing how we should act and doing so are not the same. Spiritual evolution is a function of choice, the repetition of which defines its degree.

Each time we decide not to forgive, it becomes harder for us to do so the next time: we reinforce the energy pattern defined by our emotions. Like a person in a canoe being swept into ever-faster water, our ability to reverse course and paddle back upstream continues to diminish.

The weight of these decisions is relative to the

person's understanding. Not forgiving others out of ignorance – or being taught God does not forgive– is one level of misconduct: the willful transgression of our Creator's law – knowing that to forgive is divine and then refusing to do so – carries much greater consequence.

Forgiveness requires knowledge of our progressive nature. Failure is the foundation of success: only through making wrong choices do we find the correct path. Knowing we are all in this together – one human family bound by the love of our Creator – releases us to forgive others as we would want them to forgive us: to not do so is selfish.

Our unified nature means that when someone hurts another, everyone is hurt. The side of fear gains weight: that of love loses strength. The brunt of the harm is born by the person, but through our collective consciousness we are all affected. No one can escape the suffering that is life today for more people than not.

Forgiveness is an act of love, a choice to act divine. The more we forgive others, the more we increase the quantity of love in our world: we offset the momentum of fear. The past harm done on our planet has hurt all of us: we continue to suffer the effects of it today. This bank of horror is the fulcrum that will allow us to leverage more love into our world.

People often do bad things believing their actions are correct. Their intentions do not reduce the wrongness of the act, but they do mitigate the spiritual consequences. Those who have been taught that God desires us to kill people who believe differently, are – as they best understand it - still doing God's will. Their loyalty to our Creator is not the problem, but rather their understanding of God's attributes.

We forgive others because God wants us to forgive them: this is our Creator's will. God wants everyone to achieve eternal life. To forgive another person is to increase the divinity in their lives: it improves their chances – as well as ours - of accepting God's gift. To not forgive someone is to decrease the love they experience: it reduces their ability – and ours – of choosing God's will next time.

Forgiving others does not mean they get off for the harm they have caused. Not everyone chooses eternal life, but we need to pray that everyone does: those who do will at some point realize the mistakes they have made. For any of us who in truth wish to abide by God's will, knowing we have not is punishment enough.

The effect on the world's balance of love and fear

that stems from any act of forgiveness is proportional to the harm experienced by the person. Someone who suffers the direct consequences of another person's actions must reach for a much higher level of character than someone hurt within the collective whole. Still, all forgiveness adds to the love on the planet: it demonstrates our spiritual intention. This changes us.

Our universe is accessible by the spiritual at any point in the continuum. For God, there is no time – our past, present, and future are one: all human history is condensed into one instant, that creative manifestation that contained within itself all of the stuff of the material realms. This knowledge gives us insight into how we overcome the fear that has built up over the ages.

Most people love within the current scope of their lives: they forgive, or not, people within the time span they live. This limits to a great extent the love that can be generated through forgiveness: there is only so much that can happen to any one of us that requires forgiving. Staying current with forgiveness works for us, but it does not allow our world to catch up: the downward trend continues.

The people from the past are as much a part of God's family as we are. We may feel separated from them or from

God, but our Creator never feels this. Hating people from before adds to the negativity on the planet: it works against us. Forgiving those from the past, however, does just the opposite: it adds to the weight of love changing our world.

Forgiving others for the harm they caused someone else strengthens our ability to forgive those who harm us: when the pain is personal, it is difficult to achieve a balanced perspective. Forgiving people of the past who have brought our world its horror gives us the space to contemplate with greater clarity. Distance allows us to learn more about the necessity of making mistakes: we become more aware of our own failings and more tolerant of others.

Forgiveness is one of the greatest spiritual tools we can use to affect the overall balance of love and fear in the world. We can each choose to be part of the solution. When we forgive the people who have harmed us in person, we improve ourselves: we overwhelm fear with love. This makes us a force for transformation on the planet.

We increase this process as we learn to forgive those who have harmed us as part of the collective whole, offsetting the fear being generated in the world today. Finally, by going further and forgiving those from humanity's past, we start to break down the accumulation of fear collected over the ages.

Every bad act that has happened in our history can be a focal point for bringing more love to the planet. Fear remains in time, but love is eternal: the more we give, the more we receive. Only love generates more than it takes. An act that hurt a thousand people in the past can be used by many more now, and in the future, as a continual source for bringing more love into the world.

From love and forgiveness stem good will. This means basing our decisions on the unified nature of humanity - past, present, and future.

Residing in love we work to develop good relationships with all people: we give others the benefit of the doubt. We treat them with the respect, dignity, and tolerance that we know our Creator would have us treat them. We do this without expectation of reward.

Good will implies a cheerful attitude: it is based in loving-kindness. This is something that we want to do, not a duty we perform. It is not just our actions that are important, but how we go about them.

This is a way of being: a willingness to live with faith that we are all siblings of the same loving Creator. We remain open, ready, and wanting to find ways that bring us closer to the others in our lives: we search for these opportunities rather than just waiting for them to happen.

As we experience the truth resulting from our individual efforts, we become stronger. Other avenues offering greater participation outside of our normal spheres of influence become more apparent. The philosophy of good will spreads through all areas of our lives: we apply loving consideration to all of our decisions.

As members of the institutions directing our world, we have an obligation to participate. Those we elect need to have demonstrated a commitment to the principles of good will. No one lives their lives without making mistakes. We want leaders who have learned life's lessons through experience.

Our world is first for the common person, not that fraction of a percentage who has been gifted with so much more. Our leaders must be of us: those who have demonstrated a commitment to character in their lives, and who then offer themselves for a limited term of public office.

Politics is supposed to be a service, not a profession: allowing it to become one has corrupted our governments. The United States today is not what our founders envisioned, but rather what they fought against.

Inconsistency between what our leaders say before elections, and what they do after, must carry consequences. Transparency is an absolute requirement, not a choice for those in office.

Elected officials must be held accountable: clear, direct, and unambiguous communication should be expected. Campaign expenses need to be limited, debates open to all candidates, and the process paid for with public funds: personal fortunes can no longer be a ticket to political power.

Good will is an active process: it comes from intention. We must craft today the world we want tomorrow. What has more influence on this than how we raise our children? If we do not want them thinking war is okay, we should not buy them plastic guns to act it out.

The law of cause and effect can seldom be broken. Using violence to control our children develops fear-based personalities: love never hits, shouts, or withdraws itself. Do as I say, not as I do, is the way of the past: our children have memories and the right to critique their upbringing.

The more we integrate compassion, tolerance, and

fairness into our children's education, the greater their chance of reversing the historic effects of fear. Non-violent means of conflict resolution have to be emphasized.

Our past needs to be understood in terms of how power has been achieved, and who has had to bear the brunt of the price. Good will means teaching empathy for the billions of souls that have suffered our world's journey.

Competition has its place, but not at the expense of fair play: sports must reflect our goal of higher character, not war without weapons. Athletic ability should be encouraged, not worshiped: it is the least of our attributes. Professionals unwilling to recognize, embrace, and employ their status as role models should not be supported: with fame comes obligation.

Fear-based societies allow people to fall through the social web of support needed to care for those of lesser abilities. "I've got mine, now you get yours," is today's mantra. In many ways we are like a family that outcasts its slower children. Not only do we not assist many of these people, we make life even more difficult for them.

Those of good will could never restrict assisting the hungry, isolate the poor in ghettos, or make criminals of those homeless. To foster good will is to break down the constructs separating us from one another: the degree of charity in a community reflects its spiritual maturity.

Human dignity is what is important, not a person's ability to succeed in an ever harsher world: love never turns its back to any who suffer. Living wage must replace minimum wage. Life is our right regardless of our social status: financial success is not a function of spiritual worth.

We create good will through how we spend our money: little else offers such power to so many people who feel without it. Currency has been described as spiritual energy brought into physical form: where we direct it carries consequences. Many times these are our more difficult decisions: we have been taught for so long that the bottom line is what is most important.

Some argue we should make our money first – only being concerned if it is legal rather than responsible – and then donate as we wish: justification replaces reason. People invest in companies with bad environmental records for better returns, and then donate to the groups cleaning up their mess.

Business for the sake of business must cease: to end right, we must start right and remain that way throughout the process. Who wants to get rich selling crack to kids on the one hand, and then donating to a recovery center on the other?

Owning stock means having equity in the company. This is an investment, not savings: ownership carries responsibility.

There are those companies that support life on our planet through their products, their environmental practices, and how they treat their employees: then there are those that do otherwise. Good will requires we know where our money is going and how it is being spent.

Resources are unevenly distributed across our world: we require a global economic system. To date, the wealthy nations have set the game against those less developed. This unfairness drives the poverty in the world: it increases the distance between the rich and the poor. Power based in fear, greed, and corruption never relinquishes itself: for it, exercising good will is not an option.

Supporting our local communities is also important. We are obligated to buy, work, and participate where we live to the best extent we can. Viewing everything in terms of cost is selfish: it reduces us to an economic model and steals our ability to choose love over fear. Our neighbors deserve our business before big national chains: the slight increase in expense buys the social capital bonding the community.

Good will dictates our interaction with the planet. We are expected to be fair. We are to share our world with those people living now, as well as our future generations: parents do not have a greater right to the world's resources than their children.

Business interests have promoted unsustainable consumerism in the quest for profit: they have hooked our population on this, its most deadly drug. To survive we must reverse the trend: mainlining capitalism has almost killed us.

Most people need much less: life is about our relationships, not our possessions. The fewer things we want, the less we have to work: we have more time for family, friends, and community. Buying less reduces our debt, the slavery of our times. This is the most direct way we can limit our personal draw on the planet's resources.

Next in importance is reusing what we have: care for our property was once considered responsible. Buying second hand reduces our footprint even further. Recycling, for all of its worth, remains the least of the environmental trilogy.

Our Tools for Change 59

Our world is at a point of crisis, but we have options: the future does not have to be dictated by the past. Love, if exercised, will always prevail over fear. The warmongers among us are few. With trust, courage, and new global leadership we can guide our world to a higher state of being - one that will allow us to usher in the era of peace. The choice is ours: every decision counts. Regardless of the outcome, we, the common people are responsible.

Part 4

Application of Principles: The Arab-Israeli Conflict

The conflict between Israel and neighboring Muslims continues to threaten global security, while the Palestinians remain without hope, homes, or country. Achieving a lasting peace will require different approaches than those used to date: all sides bear fault. While resolution must occur based on today's borders, clarity regarding the past is essential.

The consequences of further war in the Middle East are not acceptable. The international community deserves resolution, and if necessary, the right to direct the process. To not allow third party intervention is to put the lesser before the greater - the desires of a few before the future of the rest. Our planet must adapt to survive: anarchy as world order no longer works.

This proposal is not a detailed plan for peace, but rather an exploration into the environment required for non-violence. It is the people who are being hurt, not their leaders, and until the issues are addressed at their level little progress can be envisioned. Governments maneuver to sign treaties based on power relationships, but lasting peace only resides in the hearts of the citizens.

Problems of great complexity are best addressed when broken down to their most basic construct. The people with the least in the society – those without hope, education, or employment – have to relate to and contribute to the process. When they who have borne the steepest price over the years - and who continue to suffer today - come to terms with the past, then peace will have meaning, but not before.

Peace is an effect, not a cause: the result of love-based actions not fear inspired reactions. Hate, anger, and intolerance – the emotions that fuel the cycles of revenge - must be replaced with trust, empathy, and compassion – the feelings that lead to forgiveness. People are expected to admit their mistakes and apologize, as well as stop any harm they continue to cause. When sincere, an apology must be accepted, and the anger dropped: we all make mistakes and if we ever expect to be forgiven ourselves – either by God or our peers – then we in turn have an obligation to forgive.

This ability involves personal growth; ascending from the animal to the divine. While the greatest of our race have forgiven others even as they persecuted them, this level of conduct is beyond most people. To expect a person born and raised under oppression to develop this attribute quickly is unreasonable. Patience must be exercised. Everyone deserves the time to develop: it is why we are here. Even so, some people will never forgive. They will, though, eventually die off - only that of love has eternal reality.

Over time, good will fosters greater trust. While those who initiated the process may continue to struggle with their emotions, the next generation growing into a different environment finds cooperation easier: peace, not war, is our natural state. When the cycles of revenge have been broken, love – the only self-perpetuating energy we know - begins its healing affect. For the first time, non-violence becomes possible.

Most people lack the facts leading up to the Middle East conflict, and are afraid to ask for them. Emotions continue to dominate the issue, not critical reasoning. Any slip of the tongue draws tremendous criticism: those who enter the debate are often the target of accusations and character assassination. Many other people feel the problem is so huge, complex, and mired in religious dogma that it can never be resolved.

Reconciliation first requires an historical understanding of the events - and if needed, addressing those past actions: attempting to stop this critical review shows fear of fault. Clarity is essential: lack of transparency often means manipulation of the process and breeds distrust. While obscurity helps maintain the status quo, it will not lead to peace.

No longer is questioning the correctness of how Israel became a state synonymous with disputing the country's right to exist. While this may have been the case when the original occupation happened, time has intervened:

most Israelis today were not part of the events that happened in 1948. Tying these two concepts together – especially in a world where some people continue to call for the destruction of Israel – leaves the truth compromised and undermines Israeli security.

The reason's given to justify the original partition of Palestine need to be examined, and determination made as to their validity under international law. We know the Jews were the original aggressors: was this right, and if not, what should they do to make up for it? Only through review can appropriate responses – actions necessary to appease the people who have borne the brunt of the conflict - be mandated. World federalism is required: from this point peace can evolve.

The ancient record is one of historical fact intertwined with religious dogma. The Jewish claim is that God gave them Palestine, and many of their faith have interpreted this as meaning for eternity. Christianity shares this history, and many of their faith believe the return of the Jewish people to Palestine foretells the second coming of Christ.

Control of the Holy Land shifted back and forth over the centuries until 70 CE, when the Romans laid siege to Jerusalem and the Jews were dispersed into Europe. Over the centuries they suffered under varying degrees of oppression. By the mid 1800's some in the Jewish community felt Europeans would never accept them, and that they needed to create their own homeland, whether in Palestine or elsewhere: this movement became known as Zionism.

The early 1900's saw Palestine under British control. In 1917 Zionist leaders persuaded Britain to issue the Balfour Declaration. This document stated British support for making Palestine a national home for the Jewish people. President Woodrow Wilson supported this declaration, even though it was counter to the principle of national self-determination that he, the next year, said was necessary for a just and stable world order.

In 1919 a group known as the King-Crane Commission was sent to the Middle East to determine the desires of the local people. It was found that the Zionist plan to retake Palestine would result in the complete displacement of all of the non-Jewish inhabitants in the region. The commission informed Wilson this was in violation of the

Palestinian's right to determine their own political agenda. Regardless, Wilson gave his nod to the League of Nations: Britain began to implement the Balfour Declaration and immigration into Palestine began.

After Hitler came to power in Germany in 1933, many Jews fled. Their options were limited: the United States would only allow about 8,500 German Jews to enter the country a year, and other Western powers also limited Jewish immigration. This situation stirred Zionists from the U.S., Europe, and Middle East to petition Britain to allow more Jews to immigrate to Palestine: they did.

This caused problems for those already living in the region. The Arabs protested for several years against the Balfour Declaration, and eventually the British government acquiesced: they issued the White Paper of 1939, which stated that Jewish immigration to Palestine was to be restricted, and then in a few years, end all together.

Stopping Jewish immigration to Palestine occurred just as the persecution in Germany became more intense. This fueled the conflict between the Zionists and British forces in the Middle East. Defying British restrictions, thousands of

Jews were smuggled into the region. The Zionists mounted an insurgency and attacks on British targets killed civilian and military personal alike. According to the British then, and under our world's definition today, this was terrorism.

At the end of World War II Britain continued to oppose the formation of a Jewish state in Palestine. The Zionists redirected their efforts and began applying pressure on Washington to achieve their goals. Another commission was sent to the Middle East to search for a solution. The result was the Morrison-Grady Plan: it called for Palestine to be divided into semiautonomous Arab and Jewish regions tied together under one State. Jews and Arabs would then collaborate on further Jewish immigration.

This was a reasonable effort, but both sides rejected the plan. The Zionists they did not want to share Palestine, they claimed the rights to all, or at least most, of the land. They insisted on unrestricted Jewish immigration, and wanted their new state to be "racially" pure: only Jewish.

The Arabs felt Palestine was a part of their region: that it should either be its own Palestinian state or attached to an existing Arab country. They felt they were being asked to relinquish their historic lands to foreigners - that for others to have a home, they would have to give up theirs.

In 1947 Britain turned the matter over to the new United Nations: yet another commission was formed. This time the recommendation was to split Palestine into two separate states: Jewish and Palestinian. The Zionists agreed to the plan, but with reservations: they wanted more land than they were being offered.

The Arabs and Palestinians still did not agree to the partition. The plan meant that thousands of people would have to be removed from their homes and off land that had been in their families for hundreds of years. They also complained that the split was unequal: that the Jews were to receive over half of Palestine, yet they represented only a third of the population.

To implement this plan, the United Nations needed the support of the United States. President Harry Truman was advised by the State Department not to agree. Instead, Truman told our ambassador to the U.N. to approve the partition. White House advisors supporting the Zionist movement then began to apply economic pressure on other nations and forced them to vote for the plan. Because of these efforts the U.N. proposal was approved, just barely, in November 1947.

War broke out between Jews and Palestinians. By the first part of 1948, the Jewish side had the advantage. Truman, after being convinced by the State Department that the war was destroying our relationships with the Arabs, decided he had made a mistake and called for the U.N. partition to end. As an alternative, he offered a U.N. trusteeship over Palestine, but this idea was not adopted.

In May 1948 Israel declared itself: minutes later Truman recognized the new state. Again, he acted against strong advice, this time by his Secretary of State, George Marshall. The Arab nations responded to the Jewish occupation by sending their armies to assist the Palestinians: they were defeated. Israeli forces took not only the land allotted them under the U.N. partition, but over 50% more. In the process over 748,000 people lost their homes and became refugees.

Within several months, the United Nations passed resolution 194, which stated that repatriation was supposed to

Application of Principles 71

be offered to all Palestinians who wanted to return to their homes and who agreed to live in peace. The Jews refused. Truman disagreed with this stance, and for a couple of years worked to persuade the Israelis to allow the Palestinians to return: they would not, nor would Israel agree to give back any of the extra land they took in the occupation. Because of this, the Arab nations refused to make peace or to recognize Israel as a legitimate state.

Since claiming statehood many conflicts have ensued. In 1956 Britain, France, and Israel invaded Egypt in the Suez War. President Dwight D. Eisenhower forced an end to the attack and made Israeli forces withdraw. A U.N. peacekeeping force was deployed to the Gaza Strip and Sinai Peninsula. This gave Israel greater security and they regained the ability to use the Strait of Tiran, which they felt was vital to their strategic interests.

Then in 1967, President Gamal Abdel Nasser of Egypt requested that the U.N. remove its security forces. This allowed Nasser to replace them with Egyptian forces. Under pressure from the rest of the Arab community, he again blockaded Israeli shipping in the Strait of Tiran. King Hussein of Jordan supported Nasser and placed his army under Egyptian control should war erupt. The Arabs knew the use of the strait was tied to Israeli survival, and that they would fight over the blockade.

These events caused the Israeli population to worry about an Arab invasion, and pressure was on the government to act. On June 5, 1967 Israel launched a pre-emptive strike. They overran the Sinai Peninsula, occupied the West Bank and East Jerusalem, and seized the Golan Heights. President Johnson, unlike Eisenhower in 1956, called for a cease-fire in place rather than forcing Israel to withdraw. The invasion tripled the land under Israeli control: these areas became known as the Occupied Territories.

In response, the U.N. Security Council passed Resolution 242, which refuted a country's right to take terrain through war. It detailed a land for peace agreement whereby Arab nations had to recognize Israel's right to exist, and Israel had to pull out of the regions it had just seized. The three nations involved, Egypt, Israel, and Jordan agreed to this, but it was not definitive enough and resulted in no land returned to the Arabs.

Application of Principles 73

The forty years since have seen more conflicts, infitadas, and various proposals for peace. For many moderates, it is the area taken in 1967 rather than the original occupation that is on the table. Yet, as time and events eventually grandfathered to Israel the original ground taken, it may be that the Arabs will have to compromise more on the Territories. Regardless, it is the events to this point that define the central issues, and from which reconciliation can begin.

The Zionist claim to Palestine is based on the Jewish belief that God gave them the land: to take it, they had to kill the original inhabitants - the Canaanites. Divine favor, though, is not admissible in a secular world order. While people can believe as they wish, no one else has any obligation to their beliefs other than respecting the right of the person to hold them. A billion plus Christians may support the Jewish claim to Palestine, but for over five billion other people occupying the planet, it means little. No one's scripture holds precedence over another's.

There is confusion about this in the United States government. In May 2006 the Jewish Prime Minister Ehud Olmert addressed the U.S. Congress and spoke of Israel's "eternal and historic right to this entire land." He went on to speak of having to give up parts of "our promised land," and to have to "relinquish part of our dream" because of an "inhumane" enemy. He received enthusiastic applause. Coming from a government founded on the principle of separation between church and state, this was inappropriate. It also shows the United States lacks the impartiality required to meditate this conflict.

Claims of having God's favor, and desires to have a "racially" pure Israel (modern genetics invalidate the concept of race – there are ethnicities, but only the human race) are prejudicial, and whether ethnic, social, or religious, prejudice has resulted in many of humanity's worse atrocities. The only hope we have of eventually removing religious antagonism is agreeing to teach that all faiths are equal under a single Supreme Being. Anything else fuels the fires of hatred, and can no longer be considered acceptable by the international community.

Democracy is more than just a voting process: the definition includes equality of rights, opportunity, and treatment for all citizens - not just those of a particular religion. To consider being Israeli synonymous with being

Jewish; to structure the laws of the society to keep the citizenship of one faith; and for the leaders to claim the country has divine favor justifying its very existence, makes Israel a theocracy, not a democratic society. Governing by divine authority abrogates justice: secular law is fundamental for peace.

Some Rabbis, understanding the problems associated with any group claiming divine favor, explain that rather than God actually giving Palestine to the Jews it is more a case of the Jewish people having a close affinity for the land throughout history. This feeling is understandable: Palestine is the seat of their religion, and for some, the entire essence of their being. Still, how does this justify invading the territory 1900 years later and taking the land from those inhabiting it then?

If this was correct, then our world has many claims to territory more valid than those of the Jewish people. Does anyone really want to argue that the Jews - after almost two millenniums away from their land - had a stronger attachment to Palestine than the Native Americans surviving today have for theirs, including the indigenous Hawaiians whose islands were stolen only a century ago? Attempts to regain past glories are holding all of us back: solving today's problem's will require sacrifice by many, but with compassion, cooperation, and remaining current we can negotiate the process.

Otherwise, we are expecting people today to pay for the acts of their ancestors. We know that parent's crimes should not be imposed upon their children: this is no different. If we wish to live in peace, the cycle of retribution must end so forgiveness can begin. Our world now – it's peoples, cultures, and borders – takes first precedence. To let the past dictate the future is to condemn humanity to more of the same. We have the right to evolve: it is time we understood our obligation to mature. Only in this way will our race reach a level of conduct where peace can result.

This concept is key to Israel's survival: the State has legitimacy, if for no other reason, than because of age. Regardless of the correctness concerning how Israel came to be, and whether or not Israel ever sincerely addresses those issues, the Jewish people living there today have an unconditional right to their country. But while this refutes those who call for Israel's destruction or whom refuse to recognize the State's existence, it does not mean those unjustly imposed upon by Israel today do not have legitimate grounds for self-defense.

Some people have justified the original occupation as compensation to the Jews for the genocide enacted against them by the Nazis. The horror of what occurred in the Holocaust is beyond description – or debate. It is easy to sympathize with those who felt they were helping the Jewish people by partitioning Palestine and allowing them to create their own home. Still, this does not justify taking land from people who had nothing to do with persecuting the Jews in World War ll.

If anyone should have paid for the Holocaust, it was the Germans – direct punishment for crimes committed. Judaism had shown the ability to adapt through the ages. They understood that the essence of their faith was in their hearts, not an ancient temple: regaining the actual territory in Palestine was not essential to the practice of their religion. Would not our world, especially the Israeli and Palestinian people, be better off if Israel had become a part of Europe - a sovereign nation surrounded by allies - rather than one that can only survive through military might?

While the justifications made for past actions need to be examined today, this is to aid us in making better decisions now, not to correct mistakes from before. Still, if the premise used to justify the original aggression was wrong, then that argument can no longer be used: otherwise, the truth remains obscured. Our world needs this region at peace: the question is not Israel's legitimacy – that is unquestionable at this point – but rather, what it will take for both an Israeli and a Palestinian state to flourish together?

To achieve relative peace, Israel has several options: kill all enemies within range, which will continue to create even more; build walls, man the barricades, and live in a state of siege, as they have done since the beginning; or finally, do what we as individuals must when we wish to resolve interpersonal conflicts – admit to past mistakes, offer a sincere apology, and commit to the good will necessary to repair the relationship. As simple as this may sound, true peace will never happen otherwise.

The cycles of violence will not stop until one side decides to no longer participate, and then follows through with the commitment necessary to hold the moral ground. Any successful effort at peace must be meaningful to the

Application of Principles 79

average person on the street, both Jew and Palestinian: they are those whom will be expected to implement the agreements made by their leaders. Each side must feel they are being treated with dignity, fairness, and justice, or the process will collapse.

This requires the Israeli government to admit that the invasion of Palestine in 1948 was wrong, and to offer a sincere apology for the harm caused to the Palestinian people. Compensation needs to be offered as warranted. This is only fair – the Jews have a nation at the expense of the Palestinians developing theirs: to not offer compensation is to not recognize the equality of all people, and this bias will sabotage any chance for peace.

Compromise on both sides regarding borders will be required: Israel has justifiable security concerns, and the Palestinians need borders that allow them to develop their state with similar potential to Israel. Consensus must be achieved: without full agreement there will not be abidance. Once decided, Israel must then provide the development assistance necessary for the Palestinians to create a viable economy as they so chose. Given the part played by the

United States in creating this crisis, it is reasonable that they also be expected to contribute aid to this process.

Will these actions by Israel stop the violence immediately? Of course not: there are fanatics on both sides who will never agree to peace. It will, though, condition the environment for it to result in the future. For the Israelis to expect the Palestinians to forgive and forget - without first admitting to being the original aggressors - is to humiliate them, and no matter what agreements the governments make, there will always remain resentment.

Repentance gives Israel the moral ground, and places the duty on the other sides to reciprocate. People respect those who own up to their mistakes and who work to correct them. Our world is demanding peace, and most people understand this will take sacrifice on everyone's part. Those continuing to advocate violence against Israel will lose support from their own people, and from the other countries that today see Israel as an occupying force. Eventually, reconciliation will occur: time will work its wonders.

Stopping the cycle of revenge is critical. This means that while Israel has the right to defend its citizens, it can no

Application of Principles 81

longer return strike for strike. Doing so is retribution – punishment – not defense. It is the way of the past, not a strategy for the future. As with personal confrontations, self-defense ends when the harm being caused is stopped: the rule of law does not allow us the right to go further. Subsequent determination of guilt and any punishment to be imposed is then levied by those whom our society has delegated to the job.

For a just world order, the same is required. Only that force necessary to stop further aggression can be warranted by any nation. Third party intervention is necessary for justice: it is the only way to insure that the concerns of all parties are fairly addressed. The international community bears the responsibility to adjudicate disputes between countries, and if necessary, enforce its determinations. If the Israelis want lasting peace, this is not an option, but a requirement.

While the conflict in the Middle East between Israel and the Muslims posses our world great risk, it can also teach us our way forward: it is in our most difficult times that we find our highest character and learn our most valuable lessons. All sides have fault, but the burden has not been shared equally – the Palestinian people continue to pay the most horrific price, and reducing this suffering must take priority.

Peace requires new leaders willing to relinquish the past, accept today's realities, and work together for the benefit of all parties. This conflict does not have to lead to Armageddon: with trust, courage, and good will, the course can be changed. That choice, though, ultimately rests with people and whom they choose to follow.

About the Author

Bob left Alaska and returned to college in 2001, earning bachelor's degrees in International and Religious Studies. Working to become bilingual in Spanish, he writes and speaks on God, religious tolerance, and our tools for abolishing war. Bob has one son and lives in Eugene, Oregon. He can be contacted at godrefined@yahoo.com.

www.ingramcontent.com/pod-product-compliance
Lightning Source LLC
Chambersburg PA
CBHW051708040426
42446CB00008B/776